WHY DO FAMILIES HAVE RULES?

THE COMMON GOOD

ERIN DAY

PowerKiDS press
New York

Published in 2019 by The Rosen Publishing Group, Inc.
29 East 21st Street, New York, NY 10010

First Edition

Editor: Jennifer Lombardo
Book Design: Tanya Dellaccio

Photo Credits: Cover hanapon1002/Shutterstock.com; p. 5 Rido/Shutterstock.com; p. 7 JaySi/Shutterstock.com; p. 9 Aphichart/Shutterstock.com; p. 11 Monkey Business Images/Shutterstock.com; p. 13 andresr/E+/Getty Images; p. 15 Steve Debenport/E+/Getty Images; p.17 Pascal Broze/ONOKY/Getty Images; p. 19 Jamie Grill/Getty Images; p. 21 Svitlana-ua/Shutterstock.com; p. 22 pikselstock/Shutterstock.com.

Cataloging-in-Publication Data

Names: Day, Erin.
Title: Why do families have rules? / Erin Day.
Description: New York : PowerKids Press, 2019. | Series: The common good | Includes glossary and index.
Identifiers: LCCN ISBN 9781538330968 (pbk.) | ISBN 9781538330951 (library bound) | ISBN 9781538330975 (6 pack)
Subjects: LCSH: Parent and child–Juvenile literature. | Children–Conduct of life–Juvenile literature. | Families–Juvenile literature.
Classification: LCC HQ755.85 D29 2019 | DDC 306.874–dc23

Manufactured in the United States of America

CPSIA Compliance Information: Batch #CS18PK: For Further Information contact Rosen Publishing, New York, New York at 1-800-237-9932

CONTENTS

Your Family Community

When you hear the word "community," you probably think of your neighborhood or town. But your family is a type of community, too. A community is a group of people who live or work in the same place and have similar values and ideas. Members of a community often care about the same things.

When you work toward the common good, it means you do things that **benefit** everyone in your community. There are many ways to contribute, or give, to the common good of your family. One way is by following your family's rules. This will help keep your family happy and your home running smoothly.

Rules Keep Order

Your family likely has many rules. You might even think there are too many. Don't get upset, though—all families have rules. This is because rules are important. Without them, there would be chaos, or a total lack of order, in your family. Chaos isn't good for anyone.

Families have rules for many reasons. One of the main reasons is because rules help keep order. With order, a family can operate, or work, better. This makes home a more peaceful place, which makes everyone in the family happier. Family members get along better when they follow the rules.

Responsible and Respectful

Rules help family members learn how to be responsible. Being responsible means you can be trusted to do what's right, such as sharing with your **siblings**. It also means you can be trusted to do the things you need to do, such as feeding your family's pet.

Rules make sure family members use good manners. Saying "please" and "thank you" are common family rules. Keep in mind that your family's rules aren't just for inside your own house. You should also follow them when out in public. Being **polite** no matter where you are is good for everyone around you.

79

When you follow your family's rules, it shows you respect your family and understand that your parents made the rules for good reasons. Following rules such as washing your hands before you eat or making your bed each morning also shows you care for yourself and your **belongings**.

Follow the Rules!

Rules help family members get along. When everyone follows the rules, there are fewer conflicts, or fights. If you break a rule, such as watching TV before your homework is finished, you'll get in trouble. Your parents might yell at you or put you in time-out. It's better for everyone if you follow the rules.

Families make rules based on what's important to them. Your family might have different rules than your friend's family. For example, your family might allow shoes to be worn inside, but your friend's family might have a rule against this. Always be polite and follow your friend's family's rules when visiting.

Happy Families

Families have rules to keep their homes and lives in order. Rules help family members get along and work together. When you work toward the common good of your family and follow the rules, everyone benefits. Your family will be happier and have more **quality** time to spend together.